RUM RECIPES 2022

LOTS OF RECIPES TO SURPRISE YOUR GUESTS

CHARLES KING

TABLE OF CONTENTS

CHINESE COCKTAIL 12
CHOCOLADA 13
CHOCOLATE CAKE 14
CHOCOLATE COLADA 15
CHOCOLATE-COVERED STRAWBERRY 16
CHRISTMAS CHEER 17
CHUNKY MONKEY MARTINI 18
CINNAMON TOAST 19
CITRUS SQUEEZE 20
CLAM VOYAGE 21
THE CLASSIC HURRICANE 22
COC AMOR 23
COCKSPUR BAJAN SUNSET 24
COCKTAIL TROPIQUE 25
COCO COW 26
COCO LOPEZ LIMÓN MADNESS 27
COCO LOPEZ LIMÓNADE 28
COCO LOPEZ PURPLE PASSION 29
COCO NAUT 30
COCO POM 31
COCOA BANANA TINI 32
COCOA BEACH 33
COCOBANA 34
COCOMOTION 35
COCONUT BANANA COLADA 36

COCONUT BROWNIE	37
COCONUT CLOUD MARTINI	38
COCONUT COLADA	39
COCONUT GROVE	40
COCONUT HONEY	41
COFFEE CREAM COOLER	42
THE COLONIALIST	43
COLUMBUS COCKTAIL	44
COMPOSITION	45
CONTINENTAL	46
CORKSCREW	47
CORUBA CANE	48
COQUITO	49
COW PUNCHER	50
CRAN-RUM TWISTER	51
CRANBERRY KISS	52
CRANBERRY MINT RICKEY	53
CREAM PUFF	54
CREAM SODA	55
CREAMY SMOOTH EGGNOG PUNCH	56
CREOLE	57
CRICKET	58
CROW'S NEST	59
CRUZAN CHEESECAKE MARTINI	60
CRUZAN GIMLET	61
CRUZAN ISLAND MIST	62
CRUZAN MAI TAI	63

THE CRUZAN SUZAN	64
CRYSTAL PUNCH	65
CUBA LIBRE	66
DARK 'N' DARING	67
DARK 'N' STORMY	68
DARK SECRETS	69
DEAD ELVIS	70
DEPAZ APRICOT COLLINS	71
DERBY DAIQUIRI	72
DEVIL'S TAIL	73
DON Q CELEBRATION PUNCH	74
DON Q CHAMPAGNE PUNCH	75
DON Q HOLIDAY PUNCH	76
DRUNKEN MONKEY	77
DUB DEVIL	78
DYN-O-MITE DAIQUIRI	79
EASTER COCKTAIL	80
THE ECLIPSE	81
EL CONQUISTADOR	82
ELUSIVE REDHEAD	83
EXTRA AND GINGER	84
FALLING LEAVES	85
FANNY'S FAVORITE	86
FIREMAN'S SOUR	87
FLAMINGO	88
FLIRTING WITH THE SANDPIPER	89
FLOR FUSION	90

FLORIDITA	91
FLUKE	92
FLYING KANGAROO	93
FORBIDDEN PLEASURE	94
FOUR SEASONS STARR MARTINI	95
FOURSQUARE PIÑA COLADA	96
FRENCH COLADA	97
FRENCH CONNECTION	98
FROSTY FRIAR	99
FROZEN BERKELEY	100
FROZEN TROPICAL SPLIT	101
FROZEN TROPICAL STRAWBERRY MARGARITA	102
FROZEN WHITE-CAP	103
FUNKY PYRAT	104
FUZZY CHARLIE	105
FUZZY MANGO	106
GANGRENE	107
GERMAN CHOCOLATE MARTINI	108
GINGER COLADA	109
GINGER SMASH	110
GINGER SNAP	111
GOLD CURE	112
GOLDEN GOOSE	113
GOLDEN SUNSET	114
STONE & GRAVEL	115
STRAWBERRY TROPICOLADA	116
SUFFERING BASTARD	117

SUMMER IN BELIZE	118
SUMMERTIME	119
SUNSPLASH	120
SUNTAN	121
SURFER ON X	121
SURF'S UP	122
SWEET SURRENDER	123
TANGORU	124
TATTOO	125
THE TEMPTATION	126
TENNESSEE TWISTER	127
THREE MILE ISLAND	128
THUNDERBOLT	129
THE TIKI	130
TIKI SOUR	131
TOMMY'S BEE	132
TONY'S NOT-YET-FAMOUS RUM PUNCH	133
TOP-SHELF LONG ISLAND	134
TOP TEN	135
TORTUGA BANANA BREEZE	136
TORTUGA COLADA	137
TORTUGA PIRATE PUNCH	138
TREASURE	139
TRIP TO THE BEACH	140
TROPIC FREEZE	141
TROPICAL BANANA BALL	142
TROPICAL BANANA DROP	143

TROPICAL BREEZE	144
TROPICAL DELIGHT	145
TROPICAL ITCH	146
TROPICAL PARADISE	147
TROPICAL TINI	148
TROPICAL TREASURE	149
TROPICAL WAVE	150
TROPICO 2000 COCKTAIL	151
TRUE PASSION	152
TWISTED ISLAND BREEZE	153
UNDER THE COVERS	154
VAMPIRE	155
VANILLE CHERRY	156
VANILLE PASSION	157
VANILLE SPLASH	158
VANILLE SUNRISE	159
VELVET ROSA	160
VICIOUS SID	161
VIRGIN-ISLAND COFFEE	162
VOODOO DOLL	163
VOODOO MAGIC	164
VOODOO VOLCANO	165
VOYAGER	166
V/XTASY	167
WALTZING BANANA	168
THE WAVE CUTTER	169
WELCOME 10	170

WHALEBONE	171
WHALE'S BREATH	172
THE WILD HURRICANE	173
WINTER IN TRINIDAD	174
WITCH DOCTOR	175
X-TREME COLADA	176
YELLOW BIRD	177
ZIGGY'S STARRDUST	178
ZOMBIE 151°	179
ZOMBIE HUT'S COME-ON-I-WANNA-LEI-YA	180
ZOMBIE HUT'S MAMA'S GONE BANANAS	181
AVOCADO SOUP	182
BACARDI DOUBLE-CHOCOLATE RUM CAKE	183
BACARDI PEACH COBBLER	185
BACARDI STRAWBERRY MOUSSE	187
BANANAS FOSTER	188
BREADED PORK CHOPS WITH HERBS	189
BURRITOS	190
BUTTERED BEETS	192
CANDIED YAMS	193
CHEDDAR CHEESE SAUCE	194
CHERRIED HAM	195
CHICKEN CUT-UPS	196
CHICKEN SALAD	197
CHICKEN STICKS	198
COCONUT RICE & DRUNKEN PEAS	199
CREAM OF MUSHROOM SOUP	201

DAIQUIRI PIE	202
FETTUCCINE A LA RUM	203
FRESH CRANBERRY SAUCE	204
FRUIT SALAD WITH PIÑA COLADA DRESSING	205
GUACAMOLE	207
HOLLANDAISE SAUCE	208
MALIBU RUM CAKE	209
MANGO FLAMBÉ	211
MARINATED CHICKEN	212
MINI-BALLS	213
MOCHA PIE	214
MORGAN'S SPICY PEARS WITH VANILLA RUM CREAM	215
ONION SOUP	217
PARMESAN CHEESE SPREAD	218

CHINESE COCKTAIL

1½ oz. Jamaica rum

1 tbsp. grenadine

1 dash bitters

1 tsp. maraschino

1 tsp. triple sec

Shake with ice and strain into a cocktail glass.

CHOCOLADA

2 oz. Bacardi light rum

1½ oz. Coco Lopez real cream of coconut

1½ oz. milk

1 oz. dark crème de cacao

whipped cream for garnish

chocolate chips for garnish

Blend with 1 cup ice. Garnish with whipped cream and chocolate chips.

CHOCOLATE CAKE

¾ oz. Whaler's coconut rum

¾ oz. white créme de cacao

¼ oz. hazelnut liqueur

splash half-and-half

whipped cream for garnish

Shake and strain into an old-fashioned glass over ice. Garnish with whipped cream.

CHOCOLATE COLADA

2 oz. rum

2 oz. Coco Lopez real cream of coconut

2 oz. half-and-half

1 oz. chocolate syrup

    Blend with 1 cup crushed ice. Serve in a tall glass.

CHOCOLATE-COVERED STRAWBERRY

1 oz. rum

½ oz. Kahlúa

½ oz. triple sec

10 strawberries

Blend with crushed ice. Serve in a cocktail glass.

CHRISTMAS CHEER

1½ oz. Newfoundland Screech rum

3 oz. eggnog

grated nutmeg for garnish

    Pour into a glass over ice, stir, and top with a sprinkle of nutmeg. Light the fire, hang the stockings, and wait for good ol' St. Nick.

CHUNKY MONKEY MARTINI

2 oz. Cruzan rum cream

1 oz. Cruzan banana rum

¼ oz. dark crème de cacao

Pour first two ingredients into a mixing glass with ice and add dark crème de cacao. Stir and strain into a martini glass.

CINNAMON TOAST

1¼ oz. Captain Morgan Original spiced rum

6 oz. hot apple cider

sugar and cinnamon to rim glass

    Rim glass with sugar and cinnamon. Add hot cider and rum. Blend with crushed ice until slushy.

CITRUS SQUEEZE

2 oz. 267 mango rum

1 oz. 267 orange vodka

Serve on the rocks with an orange wedge on the side. **80**

CLAM VOYAGE

1 oz. Bacardi light or dark rum

¼ oz. apple-flavored brandy

1 oz. orange juice

dash orange bitters

THE CLASSIC HURRICANE

2 oz. Sailor Jerry Spiced Navy rum

1 tbsp. passion fruit syrup

2 tsp. lime juice

Shake with ice and strain into a cocktail glass.

COC AMOR

1½ oz. CocoRibe rum

½ oz. amaretto

2 oz. lemon juice

maraschino cherry for garnish

Shake with ice; serve in a tall glass with maraschino cherry.

COCKSPUR BAJAN SUNSET

1 oz. Cockspur fine rum

2 oz. cranberry juice

2 oz. orange juice lime

slice for garnish

Serve over ice and garnish with a slice of lime.

COCKTAIL TROPIQUE

3 parts White Rhum de Martinique

½ part syrup of cane

1 part syrup of grenadine

2 parts lemon juice

Shake with ice.

COCO COW

1 oz. Captain Morgan Original spiced rum

1 oz. cream of coconut

2 oz. half and half

Blend with 1 cup crushed ice until smooth and pour into a glass.

COCO LOPEZ LIMÓN MADNESS

½ oz. Bacardi Limón rum

½ oz. Coco Lopez real cream of coconut

1 oz. orange juice

1 oz. cranberry juice

Blend with crushed ice. Serve in a tall glass.

COCO LOPEZ LIMÓNADE

1 oz. Bacardi Limón rum

3 oz. Coco Lopez lemonade

Blend with crushed ice.

COCO LOPEZ PURPLE PASSION

1½ oz. Bacardi light rum

3 oz. Coco Lopez purple passion colada mix

Blend with crushed ice.

COCO NAUT

2 oz. Wray & Nephew rum

2 oz. Coco Lopez real cream of coconut

¼ oz. fresh-squeezed lime juice

Blend with crushed ice and serve in a tumbler.

COCO POM

¼ oz. Captain Morgan Parrot Bay coconut rum

1½ oz. Smirnoff No. 21 vodka

2 oz. pomegranate juice

1 tsp. coconut flakes

Shake first three ingredients over ice and strain into a chilled martini glass. Top with coconut flakes.

COCOA BANANA TINI

1¼ part Malibu Tropical banana rum

¾ part Hiram Walker white cacao

¾ part half-and-half

banana slice for garnish

cinnamon for garnish

Shake and strain into a martini glass. Garnish with a banana slice and cinnamon sprinkles.

COCOA BEACH

1½ Prichards's Crystal rum

4 oz. orange juice

2 oz. pineapple juice

1 oz. piña colada mix

Blend with ¾ cup ice until slushy.

COCOBANA

1 part Bacardi light rum

1 banana

1 part coconut milk

Blend with crushed ice.

                Susan McGowan, Oddfellows Restaurant.

COCOMOTION

1½ oz. Puerto Rican dark rum

4 oz. Coco Lopez real cream of coconut

2 oz. lime juice

Blend with 1 ½ cups ice.

COCONUT BANANA COLADA

2 oz. Cruzan coconut rum

¾ oz. Cruzan banana rum

2 oz. Coco Lopez real cream of coconut

3 oz. pineapple juice

Blend with crushed ice.

COCONUT BROWNIE

1¼ oz. Captain Morgan Original spiced rum

¼ oz. hot chocolate

1 tsp. whipped cream

Pour first two ingredients into a mug and top with whipped cream.

COCONUT CLOUD MARTINI

1 oz. Tommy Bahama White Sand rum

½ oz. vanilla vodka

½ oz. coconut rum

½ oz. Coco Lopez real cream of coconut

toasted coconut for garnish

Shake with ice. Garnish with toasted coconut.

COCONUT COLADA

1¼ oz. Captain Morgan Parrot Bay coconut rum

1 oz. milk

5 oz. pineapple juice

pineapple spear for garnish

Blend 10–15 seconds and pour into a specialty glass. Garnish with a pineapple spear.

COCONUT GROVE

1 oz. rum

2 oz. Coco Lopez real cream of coconut

1 oz. orange juice

Blend with crushed ice.

COCONUT HONEY

1 oz. dark rum

2 oz. Coco Lopez real cream of coconut

1 oz. honey

Blend with crushed ice.

COFFEE CREAM COOLER

1¼ oz. Bacardi light or dark rum

cold coffee to fill

cream to taste

Pour Bacardi light or dark rum into a tall glass half filled with ice. Fill with cold coffee and cream to taste.

THE COLONIALIST

2 oz. 10 Cane rum

1½ oz. dark crème de cacao

fresh cream to top

Combine all ingredients. Add ice and shake vigorously. Strain into a chilled martini glass. Top with a layer of fresh cream.

COLUMBUS COCKTAIL

1½ oz. Puerto Rican golden rum

juice of ½ lime

¾ oz. apricot brandy

Serve over crushed ice.

COMPOSITION

2 oz. La Mauny white rum

½ oz. Marie Brizard Ananas

½ oz. Marie Brizard mango liqueur

3 oz. orange juice

Shake and strain into a tall glass over ice.

CONTINENTAL

1 oz. Bacardi light rum

¼ oz. Hiram Walker green créme de menthe

¾ oz. Rose's lime juice

¼ tsp. sugar (optional)

Stir. Serve over ice.

CORKSCREW

¾ oz. Bacardi light rum

¼ oz. Asbach Uralt brandy

¼ oz. port wine

½ oz. lemon or Rose's lime juice

Stir. Serve over ice.

CORUBA CANE

2 oz. Coruba Jamaica rum

½ oz. lemon-lime soda

½ oz. grenadine

2 oz. strawberry daiquiri mix

1 oz. orange juice

orange wedge for garnish

cherry for garnish

Blend with ice until slushy. Pour into a tall glass and garnish with an orange wedge and a cherry.

COQUITO

1 ½ oz. Pyrat XO Reserve rum

1 oz. coconut milk

1 oz. orange juice

1 egg yolk

Shake and serve in a small white wine glass, straight up. Garnish with ground cinnamon and an orange twist.

COW PUNCHER

1 oz. Bacardi light or dark rum

1 oz. Hiram Walker white créme de cacao

milk to fill

Pour rum and créme de cacao into a tall glass half filled with ice. Fill with milk.

CRAN-RUM TWISTER

2 oz. Puerto Rican light rum

3 oz. cranberry juice

lemon-lime soda to fill

lime slice for garnish

Pour into a tall glass over ice. Garnish with lime slice.

CRANBERRY KISS

¾ oz. Captain Morgan Original spiced rum

2 oz. Collins mix

2 oz. cranberry juice

lemon wedge for garnish

Stir in a highball glass over ice. Garnish with lemon wedge.

CRANBERRY MINT RICKEY

2½ oz. 10 Cane rum

2 tbsp. cranberries (fresh or frozen)

1 oz. fresh-squeezed lime juice

splash club soda

3 mint leaves

cranberries for garnish

mint sprig for garnish

In a mixing glass, muddle cranberries and macerate with simple syrup and 10 Cane for 10 minutes. Add mint leaves and muddle gently. Add lime juice, and ice, and stir. Strain into rocks glass with ice. Top with club soda. Garnish with cranberries and mint sprig.

CREAM PUFF

1½ oz. Bacardi light rum

2 oz. cream

½ oz. crème de Noyeaux (or almond-flavored liqueur)

Shake with ice. Serve in a martini glass.

CREAM SODA

1¼ oz. Captain Morgan Original spiced rum

¼ oz. triple sec

1 oz. lime juice

2 oz. pineapple juice

lemon slice for garnish

Pour into a tall glass over ice. Stir well. Garnish with lemon slice.

CREAMY SMOOTH EGGNOG PUNCH

1 bottle (750 ml) Don Q gold rum

12 egg yolks

½ lb. confectioner's sugar

1 qt. milk

1 qt. heavy cream

grated nutmeg for garnish

Beat egg yolks until light (or use your favorite eggnog mix). Beat in sugar until mixture thickens. Stir in milk and Don Q gold rum. Chill 3 hours. Pour into a punch bowl and fold in cream, stiffly whipped. Chill 1 hour and dust with nutmeg. Serves 24.

CREOLE

1¾ oz. Puerto Rican white rum

3–4 ice cubes

2 splashes lemon juice

3½ oz. beef bouillon

pepper to taste

salt to taste

Tabasco to taste

Worcestershire sauce to taste

Shake. Serve on the rocks.

CRICKET

¾ oz. Bacardi light rum

¼ oz. Hiram Walker white créme de cacao

¼ oz. Hiram Walker green créme de menthe

1 oz. cream

Shake. Serve over ice.

CROW'S NEST

1½ oz. Admiral Nelson's Premium vanilla rum

1½ oz. Arrow melon liqueur

3 oz. piña colada mix

3 oz. sour mix

Blend with ice.

CRUZAN CHEESECAKE MARTINI

2 oz. Cruzan vanilla rum

1 oz. pineapple juice

1 oz. cranberry juice

Shake with ice and strain into a martini glass.

CRUZAN GIMLET

2 oz. Cruzan white rum

1 tbsp. sweetened lime juice

lemon or lime slice for garnish

Shake briskly with ice and strain into a cocktail glass. Garnish with lemon or lime slice.

CRUZAN ISLAND MIST

2 oz. Cruzan white or gold rum

lemon peel twist

Pour into a small old-fashioned glass packed with crushed ice. Serve with short straws.

CRUZAN MAI TAI

1½ oz. Cruzan white rum

½ oz. Cruzan gold rum

½ oz. lime juice

½ oz. blue curaçao

½ oz. orgeat syrup

1 tsp. superfine sugar

pineapple stick for garnish

cherry for garnish

Pour into an old-fashioned glass over cracked ice. Stir well. Garnish with pineapple stick and a cherry. Serve with straws.

THE CRUZAN SUZAN

½ oz. Cruzan rum

1/3 oz. white crème de cacao

juice of 1 orange

Shake. Pour into a goblet over shaved ice.

CRYSTAL PUNCH

1½ oz. Prichards' Crystal rum

4 oz. orange juice

2 oz. pineapple juice

1 oz. piña colada mix

Blend with ¾ cup ice until smooth.

CUBA LIBRE

1 ¾ oz. Bacardi rum

cola to taste

¼ lime

Pour Bacardi rum into a glass and fill with cola to taste. Add lime. Stir.

DARK 'N' DARING

1 shot Alnwick rum

cola to fill

Pour Alnwick rum into a tall glass over ice and fill with cola.

DARK 'N' STORMY

1½ oz. Gosling's Black Seal rum

3 oz. ginger beer

lemon wedge to rim glass

lemon wedge for garnish

Serve in a tall glass over ice. Squeeze a lemon wedge around the rim of the glass. Garnish with lemon wedge.

                    Bermuda's National Drink.

DARK SECRETS

1 shot Alnwick rum

1 bottle of Fentimans ginger beer

lime squeeze

Pour into a tall glass over ice in order listed above. Squeeze in fresh lime.

DEAD ELVIS

2 oz. RedRum

½ oz. 151 rum (to float)

½ oz. apricot brandy

1 oz. pineapple juice

½ oz. lime juice

2 oz. orange juice

1 tsp. superfine sugar

cherry for garnish

orange slice for garnish

Blend all ingredients except 151 rum with 1 cup ice. Strain into a cocktail glass. Float the 151 rum. Garnish with cherry and orange slice. Serve with a straw.

DEPAZ APRICOT COLLINS

1½ oz. Depaz Blue Cane amber rum

4 tsp. apricot preserves

½ oz. fresh lemon juice

¾ oz. Crème Peche

1 oz. fresh orange juice

half-wheel orange slice for garnish

Shake vigorously with ice. Strain into a highball glass over fresh ice. Garnish with orange slice.

DERBY DAIQUIRI

2 oz. Whaler's Great White rum

½ oz. Hypnotiq

1 oz. lime juice

½ teaspoon simple syrup (recipe follows)

lime wedge for garnish

mint sprig for garnish

Shake vigorously with ice and strain into a cocktail glass. Garnish with lime wedge and mint sprig.

To make simple syrup: Bring 1 cup water to a boil. Add 2 cups sugar. When the sugar is fully dissolved, remove from heat and allow to cool. Store in a plastic squeeze bottle.

DEVIL'S TAIL

1 ½ oz. light rum

1 oz. vodka

2 tsp. apricot brandy

2 tsp. grenadine

½ oz. lime juice

Shake with ice and serve over ice.

DON Q CELEBRATION PUNCH

1 bottle (750 ml) Don Q gold rum

16 oz. orange juice

16 oz. unsweetened pineapple juice

1 32-oz. bottle club soda

3 oz. lime juice

confectioner's sugar to taste

Pour first five ingredients into a punch bowl over ice. Stir gently. Add sugar to taste. Serves 12 to 15.

DON Q CHAMPAGNE PUNCH

1 bottle (750 ml) Don Q gold rum

3 pineapples

1 1-lb. pkg. confectioner's sugar

2 cups lemon juice

½ cup Arrow curaçao liqueur

½ cup maraschino cherry juice

4 bottles (750 ml each) chilled champagne

Peel, core, and slice the pineapples. Crush or chop slices into a large container. Dissolve sugar and lemon juice and add to pineapple. Add curaçao, cherry juice, and Don Q gold rum. Chill 2 hours. Pour into a punch bowl over ice, add champagne, and stir gently. Serves 20.

DON Q HOLIDAY PUNCH

1 bottle (750 ml) Don Q light rum

½ cup lemon juice

¼ cup confectioner's sugar

1 cup orange juice

1 cup cranberry juice

1 cup strong tea

12 cloves

8 lemon slices

10 maraschino cherries

In a punch bowl, mix lemon juice and sugar. Add orange juice, cranberry juice, and tea. Pour in Don Q light rum. Add cloves, lemon slices, cherries, and ice cubes to chill. Serves 15.

DRUNKEN MONKEY

1½ oz. Gosling's Black Seal rum

½ oz. banana liqueur

4 oz. pineapple juice

pineapple wedge for garnish

Shake vigorously on ice and strain into a martini glass. Garnish with pineapple wedge.

DUB DEVIL

2 oz. Wray & Nephew rum

2 tsp. orgeat syrup

2 dashes Angostura bitters

3 oz. apple juice

3 lime squeezes

Build the first two ingredients over cubed ice. Top with apple juice. Add Angostura bitters and lime squeezes.

DYN-O-MITE DAIQUIRI

2 oz. rum

3 oz. orange banana liqueur

½ oz. triple sec

1 oz. lime juice

Shake with ice and serve over ice.

EASTER COCKTAIL

1 oz. white Barbancourt rum

½ oz. triple sec

1 oz. Advocaat

1 oz. orange juice

soda water to top

Pour first four ingredients into a glass over ice. Top with soda water and stir well.

THE ECLIPSE

1½ oz. Mount Gay rum

1 oz. pineapple juice

1 oz. orange juice

Shake.

EL CONQUISTADOR

1¼ oz. Don Q Crystal rum

5 oz. pineapple juice

¼ oz. triple sec

½ oz. raspberry liqueur

orange slice for garnish

cherry for garnish

Garnish with a slice of orange and a cherry.

> From the El Conquistador Hotel.

ELUSIVE REDHEAD

1½ oz. Appleton Estate V/X Jamaica rum

3 oz. Clamato or Bloody Mary mix

horseradish to taste

Tabasco to taste

black pepper to taste

sea salt to taste

Worcestershire sauce to taste

lime juice to taste

celery stick for garnish

olives for garnish

Pour into a highball glass rimmed with sea salt and/or pepper. Season to taste with horseradish, Tabasco, pepper, salt, Worcestershire sauce, or lime juice. Garnish with a celery stick and olives.

EXTRA AND GINGER

1½ oz. Appleton Estate V/X Jamaica rum

6 oz. ginger ale

orange or lemon wedge for garnish

Serve in a tall glass over ice. Garnish with orange or lemon wedge.

FALLING LEAVES

1 oz. Gosling's Black Seal rum

½ oz. Marie Brizard raspberry liqueur

dash grenadine

4 oz. orange juice

Serve in a tall glass.

FANNY'S FAVORITE

½ oz. Admiral Nelson's raspberry rum

½ oz. Admiral Nelson's coconut rum

½ oz. Arrow melon liqueur

½ oz. Arrow raspberry liqueur

splash pineapple juice

splash white soda

orange twist for garnish

cherry for garnish

Mix first five ingredients and pour into a glass over ice. Top with white soda and garnish with a twist of orange and a cherry.

FIREMAN'S SOUR

1½ oz. Bacardi light rum

1½ oz. lemon or lime juice

½ tsp. sugar

¼ oz. grenadine

club soda to top

maraschino cherry for garnish

lemon or lime wheel for garnish

Blend first four ingredients and top with club soda. Garnish with a maraschino cherry and a lemon or lime wheel.

FLAMINGO

1½ oz. Rhum Barbancourt

juice of ¼ lime

several dashes grenadine

1 oz. pineapple juice

Shake with ice and serve on the rocks.

FLIRTING WITH THE SANDPIPER

1½ oz. Puerto Rican light rum

½ oz. cherry brandy

3 oz. orange juice

2 dashes orange bitter

Stir well.

FLOR FUSION

1 oz. Flor de Cana 4-year-old extra-dry rum

1 oz. Flor de Cana 7-year-old gold rum

½ oz. fresh lime juice

½ oz. orange juice

½ oz. pineapple juice

½ oz. cranberry juice

¼ oz. simple syrup

dash bitters

2 sweet Amarena cherries for garnish

Shake with ice and strain over fresh ice into a highball glass. Garnish with cherries.

FLORIDITA

1½ oz. Bacardi light rum

1 oz. orange juice

½ oz. triple sec

Shake and serve over ice.

FLUKE

1 oz. Whaler's spiced rum

½ oz. Hypnotiq cordial

5 oz. cola

cherry for garnish

Pour into a cocktail glass over ice. Garnish with cherry.

FLYING KANGAROO

1 oz. Rhum Barbancourt

1 oz. vodka

¼ oz. Liquore Galliano

½ oz. cream

¾ oz. coconut cream

1½ Oz. pineapple juice

¾ oz. orange juice

Shake.

FORBIDDEN PLEASURE

1½ oz. Mount Gay Eclipse rum

½ fresh banana

1½ oz. Ponche Kuba

2½ oz. cream of coconut

2 oz. pineapple juice

mint sprig for garnish

Blend with ice and garnish with mint sprig.

FOUR SEASONS STARR MARTINI

2 oz. Starr African rum

2 oz. ginger ale

splash passion fruit puree

tiny dash Cointreau

fresh raspberry for garnish

Shake well with ice and strain into a martini glass. Garnish with a fresh raspberry.

FOURSQUARE PIÑA COLADA

1 oz. Foursquare spiced rum

5 oz. pineapple juice (plus more to taste)

1½ oz. coconut cream

cherry for garnish

Blend well at high speed with 1 cup crushed ice. Pour into a Collins glass and garnish with a cherry and pineapple juice to taste.

FRENCH COLADA

1½ oz. Puerto Rican white rum

¾ oz. sweet cream

¾ oz. Coco Lopez real cream of coconut

1½ oz. pineapple juice

splash cassis

¾ oz. cognac

Blend with 1 scoop crushed ice.

FRENCH CONNECTION

1 oz. Newfoundland Screech rum

1 oz. Dubonnet

lemon slice for garnish

Pour over ice and stir. Garnish with slice of lemon. Parlez-vous français?

FROSTY FRIAR

¾ oz. white rum

1½ oz. Frangelico liqueur

1 scoop strawberry ice cream

Blend with ice.

FROZEN BERKELEY

2 oz. light rum

½ oz. brandy

1 tbsp. passion fruit syrup

1 tbsp. lime juice

Shake and serve over ice.

FROZEN TROPICAL SPLIT

1¼ parts Malibu Tropical banana rum

¾ part Hiram Walker white cacao

1 part strawberry puree

2 parts piña colada mix

strawberry for garnish

banana slice for garnish

Blend with ice until smooth. Garnish with strawberry and banana slice.

FROZEN TROPICAL STRAWBERRY MARGARITA

1 part Malibu Tropical banana rum

¾ part Tezon Blanco tequila

1½ parts strawberry puree

1½ parts fresh sour mix

strawberry for garnish

banana slice for garnish

Blend with ice until smooth. Garnish with strawberry and banana slice.

FROZEN WHITE-CAP

1½ oz. Appleton Estate V/X rum

2 oz. pineapple juice

1 tbsp. lime juice

Blend with 1 scoop crushed ice.

FUNKY PYRAT

1½ oz. Pyrat XO Reserve rum

4 oz. apricot brandy

dash Herbsaint

2 oz. fresh sweet and sour

splash grenadine

orange twist for garnish

mint sprig for garnish

Shake and strain over ice. Garnish with orange twist and fresh mint sprig.

FUZZY CHARLIE

¾ oz. Captain Morgan Original spiced rum

¾ oz. peach schnapps

2 oz. piña colada mix

4 oz. orange juice

1 slice pineapple

mint sprig for garnish

Pour into a glass over ice and stir. Garnish with mint sprig.

FUZZY MANGO

2 oz. Brinley mango rum

3 oz. lemon-lime soda

orange peel for garnish

Serve in a tall glass and garnish with orange peel.

GANGRENE

1½ oz. RedRum

3 oz. pineapple juice

½ oz. melon liqueur

cherry for garnish

Mix first two ingredients over ice in a tall glass. Float melon liqueur. Garnish with cherry.

GERMAN CHOCOLATE MARTINI

½ oz. Captain Morgan Parrot Bay coconut rum

½ oz. Godiva original liqueur

½ oz. Smirnoff black cherry vodka

¼ oz. German chocolate shavings

Shake first three ingredients with ice and strain into martini glass. Garnish with German chocolate shavings.

GINGER COLADA

½ oz. rum

1½ oz. Coco Lopez real cream of coconut

1 oz. Canton Delicate ginger liqueur

Blend with 1 cup ice.

GINGER SMASH

1½ oz. 10 Cane rum

¾ oz. Luxardo maraschino cherry liqueur

¾ oz. Berentzen apple liqueur

½ oz. fresh-squeezed lime juice

2 matchbox-size pieces of fresh pineapple

2 long, thin slices of fresh ginger root

1 tsp. bar sugar

pineapple leaf for garnish

Muddle pineapple, ginger, and sugar into a consistent paste in the bottom of a mixing glass. Add the rest of the ingredients and fill the mixing glass halfway with ice. Shake briefly and pour unstrained into a rocks or old-fashioned glass. Garnish with a pineapple leaf.

Best selling 2007 summer cocktail at Employees Only, NYC.

GINGER SNAP

¾ oz. Captain Morgan Original spiced rum

½ oz. ginger brandy

4 oz. eggnog

ginger snap for garnish (optional)

Blend to desired consistency and pour into a glass. Garnish with a ginger snap for dunking if desired.

GOLD CURE

2 oz. Wray & Nephew rum

1 oz. honey

½ oz. hot water

juice of 1 lime

lime twist for garnish

Mix honey in hot water until fully dissolved. Add Wray & Nephew rum and lime juice. Add cubed ice and shake. Strain into a chilled cocktail glass. Garnish with a twist of lime.

GOLDEN GOOSE

5 oz. Brut champagne

1 oz. unsweetened pineapple juice

½ oz. Gosling's Gold Bermuda rum

pineapple stick for garnish

Mix first two ingredients in a champagne flute. Gently float Gosling's Gold Bermuda rum on top, allowing it to slowly mingle. Garnish with a slim stick of pineapple.

GOLDEN SUNSET

1½ oz. Tommy Bahama Golden Sun rum

1 oz. premium orange liqueur

burnt orange twist for garnish

Pour into a snifter over ice and mix well. Garnish with burnt orange twist.

STONE & GRAVEL

2 oz. Wray & Nephew rum

2½ oz. Stones ginger wine

Pour into a Collins glass over crushed ice and stir.

STRAWBERRY TROPICOLADA

1¼ oz. Captain Morgan Parrot Bay rum

½ cup fresh hulled strawberries

4 oz. pineapple juice

2 oz. milk

Pour into a glass over ½ cup ice.

SUFFERING BASTARD

¼ oz. Sailor Jerry Spiced Navy rum

¼ oz. vodka

¼ oz. gin

¼ oz. blue curaçao

dash cherry brandy

3 oz. sour mix

3 oz. orange juice

orange wheel for garnish

Pour into a hurricane glass over ice and stir. Garnish with orange wheel.

SUMMER IN BELIZE

1½ oz. One Barrel rum

¾ oz. guava nectar

½ oz. orange juice

orange twist for garnish

Shake with ice and strain into a rocks glass over fresh ice. Garnish with orange twist.

SUMMERTIME

1 oz. Gosling's Black Seal rum

1 oz. Grand Marnier or Cointreau

2 tbsp. fresh lemon juice

lemon slice for garnish

lemon twist for garnish

Shake vigorously with ice and strain into a martini glass. Garnish with a lemon slice and a lemon rind twist.

SUNSPLASH

¾ oz. Captain Morgan spiced rum

¾ oz. Coco Lopez real cream of coconut

1¼ oz. Frangelico liqueur

5 oz. orange juice

Shake.

SUNTAN

1 oz. Kokocaribe coconut rum

1 oz. Baileys Irish cream

Layer in a shot glass.

SURFER ON X

Equal parts:

coconut rum

pineapple juice

Agwa coco leaf liqueur

Serve on the rocks or shake as a shot.

SURF'S UP

1 oz. Gosling's Gold Bermuda rum

½ oz. Southern Comfort

½ oz. banana liqueur

1 oz. peach brandy

1 oz. fresh orange juice

dash grenadine

1/8 oz. toasted coconut for garnish

Blend first 6 ingredients with a cup of ice until smooth. Pour into large chilled goblets. Sprinkle with toasted coconut. A spoon may be necessary. If you have a flair for the dramatic, serve in halved coconut shells with all but a 1/8inch of coconut meat removed.

SWEET SURRENDER

2½ oz. Baileys caramel

¼ oz. Captain Morgan rum

1 tbsp. ground macadamia nuts

1 tbsp. shaved Godiva white chocolate

TANGORU

1½ oz. Hiram Walker tangerine schnapps

1½ oz. Malibu Tropical banana rum

Shake with ice and pour into a chilled martini glass. Serve straight up or on the rocks.

TATTOO

1½ oz. Captain Morgan Tattoo rum

Serve chilled in a shot glass.

THE TEMPTATION

2 oz. Gosling's Gold Bermuda rum

¾ oz. orange liqueur or triple sec

2 oz. cranberry juice

Shake vigorously with ice and strain into a martini glass.

TENNESSEE TWISTER

1½ oz. Prichards' Fine Tennessee rum

½ oz. triple sec

splash sweet and sour mix

splash 7UP or Sprite

lime squeeze

Serve in a medium-high glass and garnish with a squeeze of lime.

This tasty drink is featured at Cotton Eyed Joe's in Knoxville, TN.

THREE MILE ISLAND

2 oz. RedRum

4 oz. cranberry juice

½ oz. grapefruit juice

lime wedge for garnish

Mix first three ingredients in a tall glass with ice and garnish with lime wedge.

THUNDERBOLT

1 oz. Stroh Original 80 rum

1 oz. Aftershock liqueur

few drops Tabasco

Serve as a shot.

THE TIKI

1½ oz. Sailor Jerry Spiced Navy rum

2 oz. cranberry juice

2 oz. pineapple juice

splash sour mix

1 oz. orange curaçao

pineapple slice for garnish

orange slice for garnish

cherry for garnish

Shake first four ingredients with ice and pour into a Collins glass. Float orange curaçao on top. Garnish with pineapple slice, orange slice, and cherry.

TIKI SOUR

1½ oz. Seven Tiki rum

2/3 oz. lemon juice

½ oz. gomme or sugar syrup

cinnamon sugar to rim glass

Rim a chilled martini glass with cinnamon sugar. Shake sharply with ice and strain into cinnamon sugar-rimmed glass.

TOMMY'S BEE

1¾ oz. Tommy Bahama White Sand rum

½ oz. Barenjager honey liqueur

1/3 oz. orange juice

1/3 oz. fresh-squeezed lime juice

lime wedge for garnish

Shake sharply with ice and strain into a glass. Garnish with a wedge of lime.

TONY'S NOT-YET-FAMOUS RUM PUNCH

1 oz. Pyrat XO Reserve rum

1 oz. Velvet Falernum syrup

juice of 1 small lime

3 oz. fresh-squeezed orange juice

2 dashes Angostura bitters

pinch freshly grated nutmeg

pineapple spear for garnish

mint sprig for garnish

Shake with ice until well blended. Strain into a 16-oz. goblet over ice. Garnish with spent lime shell, pineapple spear, and mint sprig.

TOP-SHELF LONG ISLAND

¼ oz. Captain Morgan Original spiced rum

¼ oz. Ciroc vodka

¼ oz. Don Julio Blanco tequila

¼ oz. Tanqueray London dry gin

¼ oz. Grand Marnier

splash sweet and sour mix

1 oz. cola

Shake with ice and pour into a tall glass.

TOP TEN

1¼ oz. Captain Morgan Original spiced rum

2 oz. cola

1 oz. cream of coconut

2 oz. heavy cream

Serve over a scoop of crushed ice.

TORTUGA BANANA BREEZE

2 oz. Tortuga banana rum

1 oz. lime juice

½ oz. banana liqueur or triple sec

1 banana, peeled and sliced

Blend with ½ cup crushed ice.

TORTUGA COLADA

2 oz. Tortuga coconut rum

4 oz. pineapple juice

1 oz. cream of coconut

Shake or blend with cracked ice.

TORTUGA PIRATE PUNCH

2 oz. Tortuga spiced rum

2 oz. mango nectar

2 oz. pineapple juice

½ oz. orange juice

½ oz. lime juice

splash grenadine

Shake with ice. Serve in a tall glass.

TREASURE

1¼oz. Captain Morgan Original spiced rum

¼ oz. Goldschlager

Serve as a shot.

TRIP TO THE BEACH

½ oz. Malibu rum

½ oz. peach schnapps

½ oz. Smirnoff vodka

3 oz. orange juice

Serve over ice.

TROPIC FREEZE

1¼ oz. Captain Morgan Original spiced rum

2 oz. orange juice

2 oz. pineapple juice

1½ oz. cream of coconut

½ oz. grenadine

pineapple slice for garnish

Blend with 12 oz. crushed ice until smooth. Serve in a specialty glass. Garnish with pineapple slice.

TROPICAL BANANA BALL

1 part Malibu Tropical banana rum

½ part melon liqueur

Shake with ice and serve in a shot glass.

TROPICAL BANANA DROP

1 oz. Malibu Tropical banana rum

1 oz. Stoli Citros vodka

¼ oz. lemon juice

1/8 oz. simple syrup

TROPICAL BREEZE

1¼ oz. Captain Morgan Original spiced rum

4 oz. cranberry juice

mint sprig for garnish

Serve on the rocks. Garnish with mint.

TROPICAL DELIGHT

½ oz. Captain Morgan Original spiced rum

¼ oz. crème de cacao

½ oz. crème de banana

3 oz. half-and-half

pinch nutmeg for garnish

Shake well and pour into a cocktail glass over ice. Garnish with nutmeg.

TROPICAL ITCH

1 oz. RedRum

1 oz. vodka

½ oz. Grand Marnier

3 oz. passion fruit juice

Shake with ice and pour into a tall glass.

TROPICAL PARADISE

1¼ oz. Captain Morgan Original spiced rum

2 oz. orange juice

½ banana

2 oz. cream of coconut

¼ oz. grenadine

pineapple slice for garnish

Blend with 1 cup crushed ice until smooth. Serve in a specialty glass. Garnish with pineapple slice and a palm tree stirrer.

TROPICAL TINI

2 oz. Whaler's Paradise pineapple rum

1 oz. Burnett's vanilla vodka

splash orange juice

Stir with ice and serve in a martini glass.

TROPICAL TREASURE

2½ oz. Captain Morgan Parrot Bay passion fruit rum

¼ oz. peach schnapps

2 oz. orange juice

splash grenadine

2 oz. cream

Pour into a highball glass over ice. Stir.

TROPICAL WAVE

1¼ oz. Captain Morgan Original spiced rum

4 oz. orange juice

1 oz. cranberry juice

pineapple slice for garnish

Shake with ice and pour into a tall glass. Garnish with pineapple slice.

TROPICO 2000 COCKTAIL

2 oz. Bacardi 151 rum

2 oz. Bacardi Tropico

drop Martini & Rossi sweet vermouth

Shake with ice. Serve over fresh ice in a tall glass.

TRUE PASSION

1½ oz. Tommy Bahama Golden Sun rum

½ oz. raspberry liqueur

1 oz. orange juice

2 oz. passion fruit juice

1 oz. sweet and sour

champagne to top

Pour first five ingredients into a chimney glass over ice. Top with champagne and garnish with a fresh orchid.

TWISTED ISLAND BREEZE

2½ oz. Captain Morgan Parrot Bay pineapple rum

2 oz. grapefruit juice

splash cranberry juice

2 oz. pineapple juice

pineapple slice for garnish

Pour into a highball glass over ice and stir. Garnish with pineapple slice.

UNDER THE COVERS

1 oz. Gosling's Black Seal rum

½ oz. bourbon

½ oz. Galliano

4–5 oz. hot chocolate

2 oz. heavy cream

grated chocolate for sprinkling

Pour first three ingredients into a heat-proof Irish coffee mug and stir. Add the hot cocoa. Float cream on top and sprinkle with grated chocolate.

VAMPIRE

2 oz. Cruzan vanilla rum

2 oz. lemon-lime soda

splash grenadine

Pour Cruzan vanilla rum into a highball glass over ice. Fill with lemon-lime soda and top with grenadine.

VANILLE CHERRY

1 oz. Whaler's Vanille rum

juice of 1 lime

½ oz. triple sec

½ oz. cherry-flavored brandy

orange wedge for garnish

Shake with ice and pour into a chilled cocktail glass. Garnish with orange wedge.

VANILLE PASSION

1 oz. Whaler's Vanille rum

1 oz. passion fruit juice

3 oz. orange juice

1 oz. Midori melon liqueur

Serve over ice.

VANILLE SPLASH

1½ oz. Whaler's Vanille rum

5 oz. pineapple juice

lime squeeze

cherries for garnish

Mix and pour into a margarita glass or a cocktail glass over ice. Garnish with cherries.

VANILLE SUNRISE

1 oz. Whaler's Vanille rum

4 oz. orange juice

1 oz. grenadine

Mix and pour into a Collins glass over ice.

VELVET ROSA

12/3 oz. Tommy Bahama White Sand rum

1/3 oz. peach schnapps

1 oz. cranberry juice

champagne to top

Shake first three ingredients quickly with ice. Strain into a chilled glass and top with champagne. Stir quickly and garnish with a small flower.

VICIOUS SID

1½ oz. Puerto Rican light rum

½ oz. Southern Comfort

½ oz. Cointreau or triple sec

1 oz. lemon juice

dash bitters

Shake with ice. Serve over ice.

VIRGIN-ISLAND COFFEE

1 oz. VooDoo spiced rum

1 oz. Kahlúa

½ oz. cream

5 oz. hot coffee

whipped cream to top

Pour first three ingredients into a mug. Fill with coffee and top with whipped cream.

VOODOO DOLL

2 oz. VooDoo spiced rum

4 oz. Rockstar energy drink

lemon for garnish

Mix in a tall glass over ice. Garnish with lemon.

VOODOO MAGIC

2 oz. VooDoo spiced rum

Equal parts:

   7UP

   sweet and sour mix

splash cranberry juice

squeeze of lemon

Shake first three ingredients with ice. Add cranberry juice and a big squeeze of lemon. Serve as a shot.

VOODOO VOLCANO

1 oz. VooDoo spiced rum

1 oz. Kahlúa

½ oz. cream

Shake with ice. Strain into a shot glass and shoot it!

VOYAGER

1½ oz. Captain Morgan Original spiced rum

¼ oz. créme de banana

6 oz. hot apple cider

Pour the cider into a mug. Stir in the Captain Morgan Original spiced rum and crème de banana.

V/XTASY

2 oz. Appleton Estate V/X Jamaica rum

1½ oz. triple sec

½ oz. orange juice

1 oz. pineapple juice

¼ oz. grenadine

cherry or orange slice for garnish

Fill shaker halfway with ice. Add Appleton Estate V/X Jamaica rum, then grenadine, orange juice, and pineapple juice. Finally, add the triple sec and shake vigorously. Pour into a tall glass. Top with cherry or orange slice.

WALTZING BANANA

1 part Malibu Tropical banana rum

1 part blue curaçao

pineapple juice to fill

Serve over ice.

THE WAVE CUTTER

1½ oz. Mount Gay rum

1 oz. cranberry juice

1 oz. orange juice

Shake.

WELCOME 10

2 oz. 10 Cane rum

4 chunks fresh pineapple

fresh ginger to taste

splash fresh-squeezed lime juice

splash simple syrup

1 tsp. sugar in the raw

1 oz. pineapple juice

In a highball glass, muddle the pineapple, ginger, sugar in the raw, lime juice, and simple syrup. Add ice cubes, 10 Cane rum, and pineapple juice. Stir and garnish with a pineapple leaf.

WHALEBONE

1 oz. Tanduay 5 Years Rhum (or Tanduay Dark Rhum)

¼ oz. grenadine

½ oz. lemon juice

2 oz. soda water

juice of ½ lime or calamansi

pineapple slice for garnish

½ calamansi for garnish

red cherry for garnish

Stir with cracked ice and serve in an 8-oz. highball glass. Garnish with a slice of pineapple, a shell or half of a calamansi, and a red cherry.

WHALE'S BREATH

1 oz. Whaler's spiced rum

1 oz. cranberry juice

4 oz. orange juice

lime wedge for garnish

Mix with ice and pour into a glass over ice. Garnish with lime wedge.

THE WILD HURRICANE

1 oz. Wray & Nephew rum

1 oz. Appleton V/X rum

1 oz. Appleton white rum

¼ oz. orange curaçao

¼ oz. apricot brandy

¼ oz. fresh lime juice

3 oz. fresh orange juice

3 oz. pineapple juice

3 oz. grenadine syrup

1/8 oz. peeled banana

banana slice for garnish

Shake sharply with ice and strain into a glass with fresh ice. Garnish with banana slice.

WINTER IN TRINIDAD

1½ oz. 10 Cane rum

½ oz. Navan

2 oz. half-and-half

1 tbsp. powdered sugar

cinnamon for garnish

Combine 10 Cane, Navan, half-and-half, and powdered sugar in a mixing glass. Add ice and shake vigorously. Strain into a chilled martini glass. Garnish with ground cinnamon.

WITCH DOCTOR

1½ oz. VooDoo spiced rum

5 oz. Dr. Pepper

fresh lime for garnish

Pour VooDoo spiced rum into a glass over ice, top with Dr. Pepper, and stir. Garnish with a fresh lime.

X-TREME COLADA

2 oz. Appleton Estate V/X Jamaica rum

2 oz. pineapple juice

¾ oz. sweet cream

¾ oz. cream of coconut

pineapple wedge for garnish

Blend with 1 scoop crushed ice. Serve in a colada or rocks glass. Garnish with pineapple wedge.

YELLOW BIRD

1¾ oz. Bacardi rum

¼ oz. Liquore Galliano

¼ oz. Hiram Walker crème de banana

2 oz. pineapple juice

2 oz. orange juice

Shake with ice and serve in a tall glass.

ZIGGY'S STARRDUST

2 oz. Starr African rum

1 oz. pineapple juice

1 oz. orange juice

splash sweet and sour

splash grenadine

lemon juice to rim glass

sugar to rim glass

Coat the rim of a martini glass with lemon juice. Place sugar on a plate and dip the rim of the glass in the sugar. Shake first four ingredients with ice and strain into the sugar-rimmed martini glass. Slowly pour a splash of grenadine into the glass so that it sinks to the bottom, creating a multicolored layer.

ZOMBIE 151°

1 oz. Gosling's Gold Bermuda rum

1 oz. Gosling's Black Seal rum

1 oz. apricot brandy

½ oz. triple sec (or Cointreau)

½ oz. grenadine

2 oz. orange juice

2 oz. sour mix

1/8 oz. Rose's lime juice

½ oz. Gosling's Black Seal 151°

lemon slice for garnish

lime slice for garnish

Shake first eight ingredients in a large mixing glass 3/4 filled with cracked ice. Strain into a large Collins or highball glass. Top with Gosling's Black Seal 151°. Garnish with a slice each of lemon and lime.

ZOMBIE HUT'S COME-ON-I-WANNA-LEI-YA

2 parts Malibu Tropical banana rum

½ part Malibu passion fruit rum

splash pineapple juice

Shake and strain into shot glasses.

ZOMBIE HUT'S MAMA'S GONE BANANAS

1 part Malibu Tropical banana rum

½ part Malibu coconut rum

club soda to fill

splash grenadine

cherry for garnish

Serve with ice and garnish with cherry.

AVOCADO SOUP

¼ cup Puerto Rican rum

1 large (or 2 medium) ripe avocados, peeled, seeded, and chopped

1 cup chicken stock or broth

1 cup heavy cream

¼ cup lemon juice

salt and white pepper to taste

Blend first five ingredients until smooth. Season with salt and pepper to taste. Serve cold. Serves 4.

BACARDI DOUBLE-CHOCOLATE RUM CAKE

1 cup Bacardi dark rum

1 pkg. (18½ oz.) chocolate cake mix

1 pkg. chocolate instant pudding and pie filling

¾ cup water

½ cup vegetable oil

4 eggs

12 oz. semisweet chocolate, chopped

1 cup raspberry preserves

2 tbsp. shortening

1 oz. vanilla baking bar

Preheat oven to 350°F. Combine cake mix, pudding, eggs, ½ cup of the Bacardi dark rum, water, and oil in large mixing bowl. Using an electric mixer, beat at low speed until moistened. Beat at medium speed 2 minutes. Stir in 1 cup of chocolate pieces. Pour batter into greased 12-cup bundt pan or 10-inch tube pan. Bake 50 to 60 minutes until cake tests done. Cool in pan 15 minutes. Remove from pan; cool on rack.

In a small saucepan, heat raspberry preserves and remaining ½ cup Bacardi dark rum. Strain through a sieve to remove seeds. Place cake on a serving plate. Prick surface of cake with a fork. Brush raspberry glaze evenly over cake, allowing cake to absorb glaze. Repeat until all glaze has been absorbed.

In a bowl, combine remaining 1 cup chocolate pieces and shortening. Microwave on high 1 minute or until melted. Stir until smooth. Or, heat mixture over hot (not boiling) water until chocolate melts and mixture is smooth. Spoon chocolate icing over cake. Let stand 10 minutes. In a small bowl, combine vanilla baking bar and 1 tsp. water. Microwave on high 30 seconds or until melted. Or, melt over hot (not boiling) water. Drizzle on top of chocolate icing.

BACARDI PEACH COBBLER

For peach cobbler:

½ cup Bacardi light rum

6 cups peeled and sliced peaches or 2 20-oz. packages frozen peaches, thawed

½ cup brown sugar

3 tbsp. cornstarch

1 tbsp. lemon juice

2 tsp. butter

1 cup chopped walnuts

For streusel topping (optional):

1 cup biscuit mix

½ cup rolled oats

½ cup brown sugar

4 tbsp. margarine

½ tsp. cinnamon

To make peach cobbler:

Preheat oven to 375°F. In a large bowl, combine peaches, Bacardi light rum, brown sugar, cornstarch, lemon juice, and walnuts. Place in an oven-proof casserole dish. Dot with margarine. Set aside.

To make streusel topping:

In a small bowl, combine all topping ingredients. Working quickly with your fingers, mix until it resembles coarse meal.

To assemble:

Sprinkle streusel topping over peaches and bake for 45 minutes. Serve warm. If desired, top with vanilla or rum raisin ice cream.

BACARDI STRAWBERRY MOUSSE

½ cup Bacardi light rum

1 10-oz. pkg. frozen strawberries, thawed

1 cup sugar

2 pkgs. unflavored gelatin

2½ cups whipping cream, divided

½ cup water

Soften gelatin in ½ cup water. Heat over low heat until gelatin is dissolved. Cool to room temperature. Puree strawberries in food processor or blender. Add sugar and mix well. Add cooled gelatin and stir well. Place mixture in refrigerator until it starts to set. Whip 1½ cups of whipping cream. Remove strawberry mixture from refrigerator; add Bacardi light rum and mix well. Fold in whipped cream. Pour in a 2-quart soufflé dish or serving bowl. Refrigerate. When firm, decorate with remaining cream, whipped (1 cup), and fresh sliced strawberries. Serves 4 to 6.

BANANAS FOSTER

¼ cup (½ stick) butter

1 cup brown sugar

½ tsp. cinnamon

¼ cup banana liqueur

4 bananas, cut in half lengthwise and then halved

¼ cup dark rum

4 scoops vanilla ice cream

Combine butter, sugar, and cinnamon in a flambé pan or skillet. Place the pan over low heat either on an alcohol burner or on top of the stove and cook, stirring, until the sugar dissolves. Stir in the banana liqueur, then place the bananas in the pan. When the banana sections soften and begin to brown, carefully add the rum. Continue to cook the sauce until the rum is hot, then tip the pan slightly to ignite the rum. When the flames subside, lift the bananas out of the pan and place four pieces over each portion of ice cream. Generously spoon warm sauce over the top of the ice cream and serve immediately.

        Thanks to Brennan's, New Orleans, LA.

BREADED PORK CHOPS WITH HERBS

¼ cup Puerto Rican light rum

8 thin pork chops

½ cup cream

2 eggs

salt and freshly ground pepper

1 tsp. sweet basil

1 tsp. marjoram

1 tsp. oregano

seasoned bread crumbs

olive oil

Clean and trim the pork chops of any excess fat. Mix cream, Puerto Rican light rum, eggs, salt, pepper, sweet basil, marjoram, and oregano together. Dip each piece of pork in the cream mixture and then dredge in the seasoned bread crumbs. Heat the oil in a skillet and brown the chops on both sides. Cover and simmer until well done. Serves 4.

BURRITOS

¼ cup Bacardi light rum

1½ lbs. ground meat

¼ cup onion, finely chopped

1 tsp. salt

¼ tsp. freshly ground pepper

½ tsp. garlic powder

1 tbsp. chili powder

Tomato sauce (see below)

12 7-inch flour tortillas

1½ cups refried beans

oil for frying

Cook ground meat in a skillet until well browned. Add onion and season well with salt, pepper, garlic powder, and chili powder. Mix in Bacardi light rum and tomato sauce and continue to cook until well heated. Spread some of the refried beans on each of the tortillas and place a large spoonful of the meat mixture to one side. Fold the ends of the tortilla so that they cover the meat mixture and then roll the tortillas, starting with the side with the meat mixture. Place the burritos flap-side down in a skillet with oil and fry for several minutes. Turn so that all sides are evenly cooked. Remove from the pan and drain on paper towels. Serve immediately.

For tomato sauce:

2 tbsp. olive oil

½ medium onion, finely chopped

1 clove garlic, minced

½ tsp. dried basil

1 28-oz. can whole tomatoes, including juice, shredded with fingers

salt and freshly ground pepper to taste

Heat olive oil in a large skillet over medium heat. Add chopped onion and stir to coat. Reduce heat to low and cook until translucent. Add minced garlic and cook for 30 seconds. Add tomatoes and basil; season with salt and pepper. Bring to a low simmer, reduce heat to low, and cook uncovered until thickened, about 15 minutes.

BUTTERED BEETS

½ cup Puerto Rican light rum

2 16-oz. cans whole baby beets with liquid

¼ cup brown sugar

¼ cup butter (½ stick)

¼ cup raisins

Preheat oven to 325°F. Place beets and liquid in an ovenproof casserole dish. Sprinkle with brown sugar and add butter and Bacardi light rum. Add raisins. Cover and bake for approximately 20 minutes. Serves 6 to 8.

CANDIED YAMS

1 cup Bacardi light rum

2 28-oz. cans yams, drained

½ -¾ cups brown sugar

½ tsp. nutmeg

3 tbsp. butter

1 cup orange juice

1 11-oz. can mandarin oranges

2 cups miniature marshmallows

Preheat oven to 350°F. Place yams in a large ovenproof casserole serving dish. Sprinkle brown sugar and nutmeg over the yams. Place butter in three areas of the dish. Pour orange juice over all. Place mandarin oranges over the top of the yams. Add Bacardi light rum. Sprinkle miniature marshmallows evenly over and around the top of the dish. Bake for 20 to 30 minutes or until the yams are thoroughly heated and the marshmallows melted. Serves 6 to 8.

CHEDDAR CHEESE SAUCE

2 tbsp. Bacardi light rum

1 tbsp. butter

1 tbsp. flour

½ cup milk

1 cup grated cheddar cheese

salt and white pepper, to taste

¼ tsp. dry mustard

Melt the butter in a saucepan and slowly stir in the flour until a roux is formed. Mix the milk and Bacardi light rum together. Slowly pour the mixture into the roux, stirring constantly with a wire whisk. When all of the milk mixture has been used, begin to add the cheddar cheese, a little at a time. Continue to stir the mixture as the cheese is added to keep the sauce fluid and smooth. Season with salt, white pepper, and dry mustard. Continue to stir and cook the sauce until slightly thickened.

CHERRIED HAM

½ cup Bacardi light rum

4 slices precooked ham, ½ - to 1-inch thick

3 tbsp. butter

½ tsp. dry mustard

ground cloves to taste

1 16-oz. can pitted cherries, drained and liquid reserved

1 tbsp. cornstarch

Clean and trim the ham slices of any excess fat. Melt butter in a large skillet and add Bacardi light rum, dry mustard, and ground cloves. Add cherries and a little of the reserved liquid. Place ham slices in the sauce and cook until the meat is heated through. Mix cornstarch with some of the reserved liquid and slowly add the mixture to the sauce until it begins to thicken. Adjust the seasoning to taste. Serve sauce and cherries warm over the ham slices. Serves 4.

CHICKEN CUT-UPS

¼ cup Puerto Rican light rum

¼ cup melted butter

¼ cup orange juice

½ tsp. grated orange rind

½ tsp. salt

1/8 tsp. ground ginger

1/8 tsp. pepper

1 garlic clove, crushed

1 lb. cut-up fryer chicken

Preheat oven to 350°F. Combine all liquids and seasonings. Brush chicken parts generously with the mixture. Arrange the chicken pieces skin-side up in a shallow baking pan, basting occasionally with the remaining mixture. Bake 1 hour or until golden and tender. Serves 4.

CHICKEN SALAD

1/8 cup Bacardi light rum

1 cup mayonnaise

1/8 cup sweet relish

1/8 cup catsup

2 cups cooked chicken

1 cup diced celery

½ head lettuce or avocado shells

dash paprika

8 pimento pieces

Mix first four ingredients in a bowl. Add the chicken and celery. Chill in the refrigerator before serving. Serve on a bed of lettuce or in avocado shells. Garnish with a sprinkle of paprika and pieces of pimento. Serves 4.

CHICKEN STICKS

3 tbsp. Bacardi dark rum

12 chicken wings

2/3 cup seasoned bread crumbs

1 oz. butter or margarine

salt and pepper, to taste

Cut chicken wings in half with a sharp knife. Place them in a shallow pan. Drizzle Bacardi dark rum over wings. Cover and chill for several hours, turning wings once or twice. Roll wings in the seasoned bread crumbs, coating well. Sauté in butter or margarine for 18 to 20 minutes. Sprinkle with salt and pepper. Makes 24 pieces.

COCONUT RICE & DRUNKEN PEAS

¼ cup Mount Gay Eclipse rum

1 cup dried red kidney beans (6 ½ oz.)

4 cups water

2 cans coconut milk

2 cups boiling water

5 tsp. kosher salt

2 scallions, trimmed and left whole

2 fresh thyme sprigs

1 whole green Scotch bonnet pepper or habanero chile

5 cups water

4 cups long-grain rice (not converted)

Simmer kidney beans in 4 cups water in a 5-quart saucepan, covered, until beans are almost tender, about 1¼ hours (do not drain). When almost tender, add Mount Gay Eclipse rum and let soak. Stir 1 can coconut milk into almost tender beans along with salt, scallions, thyme, and Scotch bonnet pepper or habanero chile, then simmer, covered, for 15 minutes.

Add 4½ cups water and bring to a boil. Stir in rice and return to a boil, then stir in second can of coconut milk. Cover. Reduce heat to low and cook until water is absorbed and rice is tender, about 20 minutes. Remove from heat and let stand, covered, for 10 minutes, then fluff with a fork. Discard scallions, thyme, and chile. Makes 10 to 12 side-dish servings.

CREAM OF MUSHROOM SOUP

¼ cup Bacardi light rum

½ lb. chopped mushrooms

¼ cup chopped onion

¼ cup chopped celery

5 cups chicken stock or broth

4 tbsp. butter

¼ cup flour

1 cup cream

salt and freshly ground pepper to taste

Place mushrooms, onion, and celery in a saucepan with chicken stock or broth and simmer for 20 minutes. Remove from heat and allow to cool slightly, then blend the ingredients into a puree. Return the soup to heat. Knead butter and flour together and whisk into the soup to thicken it. Add cream and season with salt and pepper to taste. Add Bacardi light rum and stir thoroughly, allowing the soup to simmer until heated through. Serves 4 to 6.

DAIQUIRI PIE

1/3 cup Puerto Rican light rum

1 pkg. (4-serving size) Jell-O brand lemon instant pudding and pie filling

1 3-oz. pkg. Jello-O lime-flavored gelatin

1/3 cup sugar

2½ cups water

2 eggs, slightly beaten

2 cups Cool Whip non-dairy whipped topping, thawed

1 baked 9-inch crumb crust, cooled

Mix pudding, gelatin, and sugar in a saucepan. Stir in ½ cup water and eggs; blend well. Add remaining water. Stir over medium heat until mixture comes to a full boil. Remove from heat; stir in Puerto Rican light rum. Chill about 1½ hours. (To hasten chilling, place bowl of filling mixture in larger bowl of ice and water; stir until mixture is cold.) Blend topping into chilled mixture. Spoon into crust. Chill until firm, about 2 hours. Garnish with additional whipped topping and lime or lemon slices, grated lime or lemon peel, or graham cracker crumbs.

FETTUCCINE A LA RUM

1 lb. fettuccine

salted boiling water

½ cup softened butter (1 stick)

1 cup heavy cream

½ cup Bacardi dark rum

2 cups grated Parmesan cheese

freshly ground black pepper, to taste

½ tsp. nutmeg

Cook fettuccine in salted boiling water until tender, approximately 4 to 5 minutes. Just before the fettuccine is done, melt butter in a casserole serving dish over low heat. Add some of the heavy cream, Bacardi dark rum, and parmesan cheese and stir thoroughly until smooth. When the fettuccine is ready, place the noodles in the casserole dish and toss gently to coat with the butter and cream mixture. Add remaining cream, Bacardi dark rum, and cheese, a little at a time, and continue to toss and mix the noodles. Season to taste with pepper and nutmeg. Serves 4 to 6.

FRESH CRANBERRY SAUCE

½ cup Bacardi light rum

4 cups fresh cranberries

½ cup orange juice

¾ cup sugar

¼ tsp. ginger

½ tsp. cloves

½ tsp. cinnamon

Clean and wash cranberries. Mix cranberries with orange juice and Bacardi light rum and bring to a boil in a saucepan. Continue to stir over medium heat and add the sugar and seasonings. Stir until dissolved. Cool until ready to serve, or serve warm. Makes approximately 4 cups.

FRUIT SALAD WITH PIÑA COLADA DRESSING

For dressing:

¼ cup Bacardi light rum

1 cup heavy cream

¼ cup banana yogurt

¼ cup pineapple juice

1 tbsp. coconut cream

For fruit salad:

5 lettuce leaves

½ cup desired fruits, peeled and sliced

½ cup shredded coconut

To make dressing:

In a medium bowl, whip cream until thickened but not stiff. Fold in yogurt, pineapple juice, Bacardi light rum, and coconut cream. Makes approximately 1¾ cups.

To assemble salad:

Arrange lettuce leaves on a large platter. Decoratively place fruit over lettuce. Sprinkle with coconut. Serve with dressing.

GUACAMOLE

2 ripe avocados, peeled, seeded, and mashed

1 tomato, peeled, seeded, and chopped

½ cup finely chopped scallions or onions

1 tbsp. lemon juice

salt to taste

freshly ground black pepper to taste

½ tsp. coriander

1 oz. Puerto Rican rum

½ tsp. chili powder

½ tsp. garlic powder

Mix ingredients thoroughly and chill before serving. Makes approximately 1½ cups.

HOLLANDAISE SAUCE

1½ tbsp. Puerto Rican rum

3 egg yolks

1½ tbsp. lemon juice

1½ tbsp. water

¼ lb. butter, melted

¼ tsp. salt

In the top of a double-boiler over (not in) hot water, beat the egg yolks until they begin to thicken. Mix the lemon juice, Puerto Rican rum, and water together and warm the mixture in a small saucepan. Slowly add the lemon mixture to the egg yolks while continuing to beat with a whisk. Slowly pour in the melted butter, a little at a time, while continuing to beat the sauce. Add the salt while you pour in the butter. Serve warm. Makes 1 cup.

MALIBU RUM CAKE

For cake:

1½ cups Malibu rum

1 pkg. yellow cake mix (no pudding)

1 pkg. instant vanilla pudding

4 eggs

1½ cups vegetable oil

For glaze:

½ cup Malibu rum

¼ lb. butter

¼ lb. water

1 cup sugar

To make cake:

Preheat oven to 325°F. Hand mix all ingredients. Bake in 12-cup bundt pan for one hour.

To make glaze:

Melt butter; stir in water and sugar. Boil 5 minutes, stirring constantly. Remove from heat and add Malibu rum. Let cool slightly before glazing cake.

MANGO FLAMBÉ

1/3 cup Mount Gay XO dark rum

4 1-lb. firm-ripe mangoes

½ cup raw brown sugar

Preheat oven to 400°F. Wash and dry mangoes. Remove 2 flat sides of each mango with a sharp knife, cutting lengthwise alongside the pit and cutting as close to the pit as possible so that mango flesh is in 2 large pieces. Make a crosshatch pattern with a small sharp knife. Grasp fruit at both ends and turn inside out to make flesh side convex.

Arrange fruit, skin-side down, in a large shallow baking pan lined with foil and sprinkle evenly with 4 tablespoons sugar. Bake in oven for 5–8 minutes until fruit is golden brown. (It will not brown evenly.) Arrange fruit on a large platter.

Cook Mount Gay XO dark rum with remaining sugar and butter in a small saucepan over moderately low heat, stirring, until sugar is dissolved. Remove from heat, then carefully ignite rum with a kitchen match and pour, still flaming, over warm mangoes. Serve immediately.

MARINATED CHICKEN

½ cup Puerto Rican dark rum

2 cups fresh orange juice

zest of 2 oranges

2 tbsp. chopped mint

1/8 oz. curry powder

½ oz. chopped cilantro

½ oz. minced garlic

¼ cup soy sauce

1 whole chicken, cut up

Combine all ingredients except chicken in a shallow baking dish. Place chicken in marinade overnight. Grill chicken, basting with marinade until done.

MINI-BALLS

1½ tbsp. Bacardi light rum

2 tbsp. soy sauce

1 garlic clove, pressed

1 tsp. ground ginger

1 lb. ground chuck

Preheat oven to 300°F. Blend the first four ingredients. Add the ground chuck and blend well. Shape into balls about 1-inch in diameter. Bake for 12 to 15 minutes, turning once. Serve with toothpicks.

MOCHA PIE

½ cup Puerto Rican dark rum

2 cups stiffly whipped cream

¼ cup sugar 1 graham cracker pie crust

½ oz. chunk sweet chocolate

1/8 tsp. cinnamon

1/8 oz. instant espresso granules

Combine whipped cream with sugar and Puerto Rican dark rum. Pour the mixture into crust. Grate chocolate on top. Sprinkle cinnamon and espresso over top, to taste.

MORGAN'S SPICY PEARS WITH VANILLA RUM CREAM

For vanilla rum cream:

¼ cup Captain Morgan spiced rum

1 pint vanilla ice cream, slightly softened

For pears:

1/3 cup Captain Morgan spiced rum

8 firm ripe pears

juice and grated peel of 1 lemon

½ cup apricot preserves

¼ cup vanilla cookie crumbs

¼ cup chopped almonds

To make vanilla rum cream:

Mix ice cream and Captain Morgan spiced rum. Freeze. Re-soften before serving.

To make pears:

Preheat oven to 350°F. Peel pears, leaving stems attached; core from bottom. Pour lemon juice over pears. In a saucepan, heat preserves, Captain Morgan spiced rum, and lemon peel until boiling. Coat pears with sauce, then roll in crumbs and nuts. Stand upright in baking dish with excess sauce; cook pears until tender, about 30 minutes.

Serve with rum cream. Serves 8.

ONION SOUP

½ cup Bacardi light or dark rum

2 onions, peeled and thinly sliced

butter for sauteing

6 cups beef broth

salt to taste

freshly ground pepper to taste

6 slices French bread, lightly toasted

grated Parmesan cheese

Gruyere cheese (optional)

Preheat oven to 275°F. Lightly sauté the sliced onions in butter until slightly browned. Add the beef broth and ¼cup Bacardi light or dark rum and season to taste with salt and pepper. Cover and simmer over low heat for 30 minutes. Stir in ¼cup Bacardi light or dark rum. Pour the soup into a casserole or 6 individual serving dishes. Place French bread (toasted slightly) over the soup and sprinkle Parmesan cheese on top. Place the dish or dishes in preheated oven for approximately 5 minutes, or until cheese has melted. Serve immediately. Serves 6.

PARMESAN CHEESE SPREAD

¼ cup Bacardi light rum

½ cup sour cream

1 cup grated Parmesan cheese

3 slices bacon, cooked and chopped

Mix the ingredients together thoroughly. Makes approximately 1½ cups.

To serve:

Spread the mixture on small slices of toast, cocktail rye bread, or small pieces of English muffin and run under the broiler for several minutes until golden.